T0113841

Kitchen Gems Cookbook Inc.

IDA MAE ROBINSON CHAPMAN

authorHOUSE®

AuthorHouse™
1663 Liberty Drive
Bloomington, IN 47403
www.authorhouse.com
Phone: 833-262-8899

Published by AuthorHouse 12/09/2022

ISBN: 978-1-6655-0722-6 (sc)
ISBN: 978-1-6655-0721-9 (e)

CONTENTS

Salads.. 1

Appetizers 9

Breads 15

Vegetables 21

Casseroles... 35

Wild Game 41

Meats 51

Seafood 63

Desserts... 69

Pies 73

Cakes 79

Preserves.. 91

SaLaDS

TUNA SALAD

---

3 cans tuna fish (drained)
4 boiled eggs
2 Tbls. sweet pickled relish
1 red Delicious apple, peeled and chopped
1/2 cup mayonnaise

Mix all ingredients at once.
Chill and serve.

APPLE SALAD

3 chopped red Delicious apples
2 chopped green Delicious apples
1 Tbl. chopped celery
1/2 cup raisins
1/2 cup chopped pecans
Medium cup Cool Whip

Mix and serve at once.

POTATO SALAD

---

5 large Irish potatoes
4 large eggs
2 Tbls. sweet pickle relish
Small jar pimentos
1/2 tsp. salt
1/2 tsp. black pepper
1/4 tsp. sugar
1 tsp. mustard
1/2 cup mayonnaise

Peel and cube potatoes.
Boil until cooked firm (20 minutes).
Boil eggs until firm.
Drain potatoes (pour off all water) and cool.
Peel and dice eggs.
Place all ingredients in serving dish and mix well.
Serve (refrigerate leftovers).

CARROT SALAD

1 standard package of grated carrots
1/2 cup raisins
1 Tbl. sugar
1 Tbl. chopped celery
1/2 cup mayonnaise

Mix all ingredients and serve.

CHEF'S SALAD

---

1 head of lettuce (any type)
2 diced tomatoes
2 sliced cucumbers
1 shredded carrot
1/2 pound packaged diced ham.
1 boiled egg
Bacon (4 crisp slices) (optional)
1/2 Cup shredded cheese
1/2 Cup Chopped walnuts

Place lettuce in typical salad bowl.
Diced tomatoes and cucumbers and add to lettuce.
Sauté 1 cup of packaged diced ham (10 minutes).
Allow ham to cool.
Mix ham into salad.
Sprinkle on: bacon pieces (optional), shredded cheese, diced boiled egg, chopped walnuts.

CABBAGE SLAW

1 small green cabbage
1 small red cabbage
2 carrots
1 small onion
1/2 cup sugar
1/4 cup vinegar
1 cup mayonnaise

Grate cabbage and carrots (place into salad bowl).
Dice onion and add to cabbage and carrots.
Add sugar, mayonnaise and vinegar.
Mix all ingredients well.
Serve.

appetizers

BARBEQUE SHRIMP

1 oz. bottle of barbeque sauce (preferred brand)
1 lb. bacon
Large shrimp (preferred amount), clean and devein
1/2 cup brown sugar
Sesame seeds

Wrap each shrimp with one strip of bacon (secure with wooden toothpicks).
Sprinkle on brown sugar.
Place in appropriate baking dish.
Cover with barbeque sauce.
Bake uncovered at 400 degrees for 20-25 minutes or until bacon is crisp.
Sprinkle on sesame seeds (preferred amount).
Serve.

MEATBALLS

1 standard bag of meatballs
1 regular jar of grape jelly
1 tsp. lemon juice
1 jar of chili sauce

Mix and Heat lemon juice, jelly and chili sauce in saucepan at low heat
   until jelly is melted.
Pour over meatballs.
Bake at 350 degrees for 20 minutes or until done.

DEVILED EGGS

---

1 dozen eggs
1/2 tsp. salt
1/4 tsp. black pepper
3-4 Tbls. mayonnaise
1 Tbl. mustard
4 slices of bacon
3 Tbls. sweet pickle relish
1 tsp. sugar

Cook bacon until crisp and crumbly.
Boil eggs for 20 minutes with salt (salt to taste).
Cool eggs with cold water.
Peel eggs and cut in half (length wise) and set aside.
Remove egg yokes, crumble and set aside.
Set egg white halves aside.
Mix all ingredients in salad bowl (except egg whites) together.
Spoon mixed ingredients into egg white halves.
Serve.

CANDIED SWEET POTATOES

---

3 lbs. medium-sized sweet potatoes
1/2 stick of butter
1 tsp. cinnamon
1 cup mini marshmallows
1 cup brown sugar

Place cubed sweet potatoes into microwave-safe cooking dish. Microwave on high for 6 minutes (or until done).
Place in serving dish.
Top with butter; sprinkle on cinnamon; add marshmallows (preferred amount) and brown sugar.
Serve.

BREADS

CORN BREAD

2 cups self-rising corn meal
1/2 cup self-rising flour
1 Tbl. sugar
2 Tbls. margarine
1 egg
2 cups whole milk or buttermilk

Preheat oven at 400 degrees.
Preheat skillet with 1 Tbl. of cooking grease.
Mix all ingredients at once.
Pour into hot greased skillet or greased muffin pan (Baker's Joy, optional).
Bake at 400 degrees until golden brown.

BISCUITS

2 cups self-rising flour
1/2 cup shortening
3/4 cups buttermilk
Cooking Sheet-Wax Paper

Preheat oven at 350 degrees.
Pour flour into mixing bowl.
Make a fist-sized depression in the flour.
Scoop shortening into center of flour.
Add milk (while squeezing into flour to make dough).
Mix into dough and knead until dough is smooth.
Spread unused flour onto wax paper or cooking sheet.
Roll out dough onto cooking sheet.
Sprinkle flour randomly as needed to keep dough from sticking to cooking sheet.
Roll and cut dough about 3/4 to 1 inch thick.
Cut with biscuit cutter.
Spray cooking dish with cooking spray.
Bake at 350 degrees about 15 minutes or until lightly golden.
Serve.

CRACKLN' BREAD

1 and 1/2 cup self-rising corn meal
1/4 cup self-rising flour
1 tsp. sugar
1/2 tsp. salt
1 egg
2 cups pork skins
1 and 1/2 cup whole milk (buttermilk optional)

Preheat oven at 400 degrees.
Cover and soak pork skins in water for 15 minutes or until soft to touch.
Remove pork skins from water.
Separate crackln' (fat) from pork skin and dispose pork skin.
Pour into mixing bowl.
Mix all ingredients at once.
Bake at 400 degrees until golden brown.
Serve.

HUSH PUPPIES

2 cups self-rising corn meal
1/2 cup self-rising flour
1/2 cup grated onion
1/2 cup cooking oil
1 egg
1 and 1/2 cup whole milk

Heat skillet with 1/2 cup of cooking oil.
Mix all ingredients into dough in cooking bowl.
Scoop dough by spoonful into skillet.
Cook until golden brown.
Serve.

VEGETABLES

BLACK-EYED PEAS

1 lb. black eyed peas
3 slices of salt pork or ham hock
Salt
Pepper
Sugar

Boil ham hock until tender and set aside.
Rinse peas with cold water in colander.
Pour peas into bowl.
Soak peas in cold water for 1 hour and set aside.
Pour 4 cups of water into cooking pot.
Add peas.
Add 3 slices of cooked salt meat or ham hock.
Boil for 45 minutes.
Add 1 tsp. sugar.
Add salt and pepper to taste.
Cook for 1 hour.
Serve.

GREEN BEANS

2 medium cans green beans
1/2 stick margarine
Salt
Pepper
1 ham hock, neck bone or 2 cubic-inch piece of country ham

If using fresh green beans, cut end tips from both sides of beans (cut to
    desired length) and dispose end tips.
Pour 2 cups of water into boiling pot.
Rinse beans and drain off all water.
Pour washed beans into boiling pot (cold water).
Add ham hock, neck bone or 2 cubic-inch piece of country ham.
Add 1/2 stick margarine.
Add salt and pepper to taste.
Boil for 35 minutes (if using fresh green beans) or until tender. (If using
    canned green beans, boil 10 minutes).
Serve.

COLLARD GREENS

3 quart-size bags chopped collard greens
4 smoked pork neck bones or 2 ham hocks
Okra (optional)
1 hot pepper pod (optional)
1/2 tsp. salt
1/2 tsp. sugar

Boil neck bones or ham hock (about 2 hours) until tender and set aside.
Rinse greens thoroughly.
Pour 4 cups of cold water into boiler.
Add rinsed collard greens and cooked neck bones or ham hocks.
Add salt, sugar and pepper pod.
Cook for 45 minutes.
Add okra (optional).
Cook for 15 additional minutes or until okra is tender.

PINK-EYED PEAS

Pink eyed peas (2 quarts)
2 ham hocks
Sugar
Salt
Pepper

Boil ham hock 1 to 1-1/2 hours and set aside.
Rinse peas and pour into boiler.
Add cold water (just enough to cover peas).
Add boiled ham hocks.
Add sugar.
Add salt and pepper to taste.
Cook on low heat for 1 to 1-1/2 hours.
Serve.

BAKED BEANS

---

2 16 oz. cans of pork-n-beans
1 cup tomato ketchup
1/2 medium sized onion
1 Tbls. barbeque sauce
¼ cup brown sugar

Preheat oven at 350 degrees.
Pour ingredients into baking dish and Stir.
Cover and bake at 350 degrees for 15-20 minutes.

RED BEANS

1 lbs. red beans
1/2 cup cubed ham
1 tsp. sugar
1 lb. sausage (smoked Conecuh sausage or red links, if desired)
1 tsp. salt
1/2 tsp. black pepper
1 Tbl. bacon grease

Soak beans overnight at room temperature.
Rinse beans in cold water.
Pour beans into boiler or cooking pot.
Add water (just enough to cover the beans).
Add bacon grease.
Cook beans until half done and add sausage (cut into one inch links) and
    cook until tender on low to medium heat.
Add 1 Tbl. sugar.
Salt and pepper to taste.
Serve over rice.

BROCCOLI

2 clusters of broccoli
1/2 stick of butter or margarine
Salt

Wash broccoli and place into colander.
Place colander into fitted boiler with 2 cups of water.
Add 1/2 stick of butter or margarine.
Add 1/2 tsp. salt.
Steam for 10 minutes.

CABBAGE

1 medium cabbage
3 slices of bacon
1 small onion
1/2 green bell pepper
1 Tbl. cooking oil
1 tsp. salt
1/2 tsp. black pepper
1/2 tsp. of sugar

Rinse cabbage.
Fry 3 slices of bacon (set aside).
Cut up rinsed cabbage (salad form).
Place cabbage in skillet with bacon (add 1/2 cup water; 1 Tbl. cooking oil; salt; pepper; sugar; green bell pepper and onion) and cook for 20 minutes, (stirring continually).
Serve.

CANDIED YAMS

8 large to medium yams or sweet potatoes
2 cups sugar
1/2 stick of butter or margarine
1 tsp. lemon flavor
1/2 tsp. nutmeg

Peel and rinse potatoes.
Cut into thin round slices and set aside.
Pour potatoes into medium-sized cooking pot.
Pour 2 cups of sugar into cooking pot on top of potatoes.
Add 4 cups of water.
Add 1/2 stick of butter or margarine.
Add 1 tsp. of lemon flavor.
Add 1/2 tsp. nutmeg.
Cook at medium heat until tender and slightly syrupy.
Serve.

FRIED GREEN TOMATOES

Green tomatoes (1 per serving)
1 cup self-rising corn meal
1/2 cup self-rising flour
1/4 cup cooking oil

Slice tomatoes 1/4 inch thick.
Add 1 cup of corn meal and 1/2 cup of flour and mix in mixing bowl.
Mix all ingredients.
Batter tomatoes thoroughly.
Place into hot cooking oil.
Cook until golden brown on each side.
Serve.

FRIED CORN

Fresh corn (shaved from corn cob) or 2 cups of canned corn (whole kernel)
1/2 stick of butter
1 tsp. flour
1/2 cup whipping cream
Salt
Pepper

Put melted butter into fryer.
Pour corn into fryer.
Add flour.
Add whipping cream.
Add salt and pepper to taste.
Fry corn for 30 minutes on low heat.
Serve.

SQUASH

---

4 large squash
1 large onion
3/4 stick of Oleo margarine
Salt
Pepper

Rinse squash.
Cube or slice squash.
Place in appropriate sized boiler.
Add largely-diced onions.
Add butter or Oleo margarine.
Add salt and pepper to taste.
Add 1/4 cup of water.
Cook on low for 45 minutes (mostly steaming).
Serve.

CASSEROLES

CHICKEN AND DRESSING

1 cut up chicken or hen
1 large pan of corn bread
1 large package of corn bread stuffing
1 cup chopped celery
1 cup chopped onions
1 diced green bell pepper
1 dozen eggs
2 small cans cream of chicken soup
2 sticks of butter or margarine
Salt (salt to taste)
Pepper (pepper to taste)

Preheat oven at 350 degrees.
Boil chicken or hen (season with salt and pepper) until tender and set aside.
Whip eggs in mixing bowl.
Sauté onions, chopped celery and diced bell pepper in butter or margarine
    and pour into mixing bowl with eggs.
Crumble cornbread stuffing mix and pour into mixing bowl with other
    ingredients and mix.
Pour chicken broth into the mix (enough broth until the mix becomes
    slightly soupy) and stir evenly.
Salt and pepper to taste.
Ingredients need to be poured into casserole dish, and drop and spread
    chicken pieces on top.
Cover with aluminum foil.
Bake at 350 degrees for 45-50 minutes.
Save some broth to drizzle on top of dressing when done.
Serve.

CHICKEN AND DRESSING GIBLET GRAVY

2 cups of chicken broth
1 cup of chicken gizzards
1/4 cup cooked boiled chicken breast (dice the chicken breast)
2 boiled eggs
1/2 tsp. salt
1/2 tsp. pepper
1/2 tsp. corn starch
3 drops yellow food coloring

Boil gizzards in chicken broth until very tender.
Add chicken breast pieces, diced eggs, salt, pepper and corn starch.
Stir slowly while cooking on low heat.
Add yellow food coloring to suit color.
Bring to a boil.
Let simmer for 5 minutes.
Serve.

MACARONI AND CHEESE

16 oz. Macaroni (Elbow Pasta)
Water
1 tsp. salt
2 tsp. black pepper
2 eggs
2 sticks of butter
4 cups sharp cheddar cheese
4 cups evaporated milk (Carnation or Pet)

Preheat oven to 350 degrees.
Bring a large pot of water to a boil (add salt to taste).
Add macaroni (constantly stir until firm; do not overcook).
Drain macaroni (run cold water over); set aside in colander.
Add 2 sticks of melted butter in large pot.
Make milk-cheese mixture (mix milk, eggs, 2 cups of cheese, black pepper in
    mixing bowl (mix well)
Add milk-cheese mixture to heated melted butter in large pan. Constantly stir
    until mixture becomes saucy (do not overcook).
Stir in 1 cup of reserved cheese into macaroni.
Pour macaroni into a casserole dish.
Sprinkle remaining cheese on top; sprinkle black pepper on top of cheese.
Bake until cheese has melted on top (approximately 15 minutes).

CHICKEN AND DUMPLINGS

1 cut-up chicken or hen
2 eggs
1/4 cup whole milk
4 cups all-purpose flour
1/2 cup Crisco shortening
1 tsp. salt
1 tsp. pepper
1 cup whipping cream

Boil chicken or hen until tender (season with salt and pepper to taste).
Remove from broth (save broth).
Cool and remove from bone.
Add whipping cream to broth.
Salt and pepper to taste.
Let broth boil on medium heat.
Pour flour into mixing bowl.
Add shortening and whipped eggs.
Add milk and make dough.
Dust hands with flour to prevent sticking to dough.
Roll dough very thin onto wax paper or aluminum foil (sprinkle flour on wax
    paper or foil paper to prevent sticking).
Cut into small squares.
Place squares (one by one to prevent sticking together) into boiling broth.
(If broth is too thin, mix 1 tsp. of flour in 1/2 cup water. Make paste and add
    to dumplings.)
Add deboned chicken
Cook until dumplings are firm.

WILD GAME

FRIED QUAIL

Two quail
Salt
Pepper
Season-All seasoning salt
Flour
Cooking oil

Cut quail into sections (breast, thighs and legs)
Season to taste.
Batter quail in flour.
Preheat oil in cooking pan.
Place quail in cooking pan.
Fry until golden

RABBIT

One cut-up rabbit
6 cups of water
Self-rising flour
1/2 tsp. salt
1/2 tsp. red pepper
Spice seasoning (optional)
1 cup cooking oil

Place water and rabbit in medium-sized pot.
Add 1/2 tsp. salt.
Add 1/2 tsp. red pepper.
Add spices seasonings (optional).
Cook until tender.
Remove rabbit from pot and set aside.
Heat skillet with 1 cup of cooking oil.
Batter rabbit in self-rising flour.
Fry until brown on both sides.

SPICY RABBIT

One cut-up rabbit
Salt
Pepper
Flour
Cajun seasoning and 2 pepper pods green or red
One chopped garlic clove.
One whole green pepper.

Season rabbit with Cajun seasoning.
Brown rabbit in cooking pan.
Remove rabbit from pan.
Pour 2 and 1/2 cups water into cooking pan.
Add chopped garlic clove.
Add one whole green pepper.
Add Cajun seasoning to mix (as needed).
Stir till mixed.

Preheat oven at 400 degrees.
Place rabbit in cooking gravy and cover.
Cook in oven at 345-400 degrees for 45 minutes to 1 hour.

SQUIRREL DUMPLINGS

3 cut up squirrels
2 bay leaves
Salt
Pepper
Water
3 cups of all-purpose flour
1/4 stick margarine
1 egg
1 cup milk
Crisco Shortening

Place squirrels in boiler with water just enough to cover.
Add 2 bay leaves.
Salt and pepper to taste.
Cook until squirrels are tender.
Remove from boiler and set aside.
Keep squirrel broth.

Dumplings:
Place flour, margarine, shortening, milk and egg in a mixing bowl and
    make dough.
Roll on wax paper, flatten very thin.
Dust hands with flour to keep from sticking.
Sprinkle flower onto wax paper or foil paper.
Cut into two inch squares.
Drop into boiling squirrel broth (one by one to prevent sticking)
Add squirrel quarters.
Cook on medium heat for about 15 minutes.
Let simmer on low for about 35 minutes
Serve.

BAKED COON AND POTATOES

1 cut up coon
1/2 cup vinegar
2 bay leaves
1 tsp. red pepper
1 tsp. salt
1 tsp. black pepper
1 stick margarine (melted)
Bacon (4 strips)
8 medium sized sweet potatoes

Preheat oven at 350 degrees.
Remove musk (non-muscular tissue and fat) from all joints.
Soak coon in large bowl in 1/4 cup salt; 1/2 cup vinegar for 30 minutes.
Place in large boiler with water just enough to cover.
Add bay leaves, red pepper, salt, and black pepper.
Boil until tender.
Remove coon from pot and set aside.
Place sliced, peeled sweet potatoes into broth or coon juice and boil until tender.
Place coon in baking dish and place cooked sweet potatoes between coon pieces.
Pour melted margarine over coon.
Cover with strips of uncooked bacon.
Cover with aluminum foil.
Place in oven and bake approximately 30 minutes or until tender (bacon should be crisp and potatoes should be brown around the edges).
Remove and serve.

DEER STEAK

Deer steak or tenderloin
Meat tenderizer
Salt and pepper
Self-rising flour
Cooking oil
1 large green pepper (optional)
Season All seasoning salt
Season steak with 1 tsp. Season-All seasoning salt.
Allow to marinate for 30 minutes.
Salt and pepper to taste.
Heat cooking oil in skillet.
Fry on both sides until golden brown on medium heat.
Remove oil from skillet.
Pour in 1 cup water.
Place deer into skillet.
Add green pepper (optional).
Cover skillet and let simmer for 1 hour.
Serve over rice or with biscuits and syrup.

DEER ROAST

4 to 5 lbs. Deer roast
1 tsp. salt
1/2 cup flour
1/4 cup vinegar
2 garlic cloves
Meat tenderizer seasoning
1 tsp. black pepper
2 bay leaves
1/4 cup Crisco shortening
2 cut up onions (sliced)
1 well-sliced green bell pepper
1/4 tsp. of red pepper (less red pepper to season to taste)

Preheat oven at 350 degrees.
Soak deer in salt and vinegar water for 1 hour.
Melt 1 cup of Crisco in roaster.
Flour roast completely.
Pour cooking oil in preheated skillet.
Brown deer roast on both sides in skillet.
Pour off excess cooking oil.
Add onions, bell pepper, bay leaves, red pepper and 3 cups of water to skillet.
Cover and bake for 2 and 1/2 hours or until tender.

PHEASANT AND WILD RICE

1 pheasant
1/4 tsp. salt
1/2 tsp. black pepper
1 Tbl. Rosemary
1/4 tsp. garlic salt
1/4 tsp. of Season-All seasoning
1/2 stick butter or margarine
1 quart sized garlic butter injection marinate

Wash and drain pheasant.
Place in roaster or cooking dish.
Add onions, bell pepper, celery and water (optional).
Season with salt, pepper, seasoning salt, rosemary, garlic salt and inject
    with garlic butter marinate (season to taste).
Let marinate overnight.
Preheat oven at 350 degrees.
Pour on melted butter prior to cooking.
Cover with aluminum foil or cooking dish lid.
Bake at 350 degrees until tender (about 3 hours).
Serve with wild rice (optional).

Meats

CHICKEN GIZZARDS

3 lbs. chicken gizzards
2 cups of self-rising flour
1 tsp. salt
1 tsp. pepper
1 tsp. seasoning salt

Rinse and boil gizzards for 45 minutes.
Roll gizzards in flour.
Season to taste.
Fry until done.
Serve.

FRIED CHICKEN

1 whole cut-up chicken
1 tsp. salt
1 tsp. pepper
1 tsp. seasoning salt
1 tsp. garlic salt
1 cup cooking oil
2 cups self-rising flour

Rinse and season chicken with salt, pepper, garlic salt and seasoning salt (season to taste).
Batter chicken in flour.
Cook in deep fryer on medium heat until golden brown.

SMOTHERED CHICKEN

1 whole cut-up chicken
1/2 sliced onion
1 tsp. salt
1 tsp. pepper
1 tsp. seasoning salt
1 tsp. garlic salt
1 cup cooking oil
2 cups self-rising flour

Rinse and season chicken with salt, pepper, garlic salt and seasoning salt (season to taste).
Batter chicken in flour.
Cook in deep fryer on medium heat until golden brown.
Pour off cooking oil (leave chicken in skillet with just enough cooking oil to barely cover the bottom).
Place ½ sliced onion over chicken.
Pour 1 cup of water into skillet with chicken and onion.
Cover with lid cover and let cook on low-medium for 15 minutes or until gravy thickens.
Add one drop of Kitchen Bouquet for coloring during smothering phase (optional).

FRIED PORK CHOPS

One package center cut pork chops
1/2 tsp. Season-All brand seasoning
1/2 tsp. pepper
1/2 tsp. salt
2 cups self-rising flour
Cooking oil

Rinse and season pork chops to taste with all ingredients.
Let marinate for 30 minutes.
Cover with flour completely.
Deep fry until golden brown.

SMOTHERED PORK CHOPS

One package center cut pork chops
1/2 tsp. Season-All brand seasoning
1/2 tsp. pepper
1/2 tsp. salt
2 cups self-rising flour
Cooking oil

Rinse and season pork chops to taste with all ingredients.
Let marinate for 30 minutes.
Cover with flour completely.
Deep fry until golden brown.
Pour off cooking oil (leave pork chops in skillet with just enough cooking oil to barely cover the bottom).
Place ½ sliced onion over pork chops.
Pour 1 cup of water into skillet with pork chops and onion.
Cover with lid cover and let cook on low-medium for 15 minutes or until gravy thickens.
Add one drop of Kitchen Bouquet for coloring during smothering phase (optional).

TURKEY NECKS

2 packs turkey necks (about 5 lbs.)
1 large onion
1 medium green bell pepper
1/2 cup chopped celery
1/2 tsp. red pepper
1 tsp. black pepper
1- 1/2 tsp. salt
2 tsp. Kitchen Bouquet

Rinse and remove fat from turkey necks.
Place in boiling pot.
Add water to cover just the top of turkey necks.
Add all ingredients (add corn starch or flour to thicken roux as needed).
Cook until tender.
Serve with rice.

MEAT LOAF

3 lbs. ground beef
1/2 lb. pork sausage
1 12 oz. can stewed tomatoes
3 eggs
1 tsp. salt
1/2 tsp. pepper
Tomato ketchup

Preheat oven at 350 degrees.
Mix all ingredients well.
Place in appropriate sized cooking dish.
Shape into loaf.
Cover with aluminum foil or cooking dish lid.
Bake for 30 minutes.
Remove from oven.
Uncover meatloaf and cover with tomato ketchup.
Slice and serve.

SHANK PORTION HAM

1 can crushed pineapple
1/2 cup brown sugar
1/2 can Coca Cola

Preheat oven at 350 degrees.
Rinse ham and place in cooking dish.
Pour Coca Cola onto ham.
Baste with crushed pineapple and brown sugar.
Cover pan in foil or cooking dish lid.
Place in 350 degree oven.
Cook for 2 hours.

BEEF ROAST

1 5 lbs. beef roast
1/2 tsp. salt
1/2 tsp. pepper
2 cups self-rising flour
1 cup cooking oil
1/2 cup chopped onions
1/2 cup green bell pepper
1/2 cup chopped celery
2 cups water
2 garlic cloves

Preheat oven at 350 degrees.
Rinse roast.
Place split garlic cloves on top of roast.
Batter roast all over with flour.
Brown in cooking oil in skillet on both sides.
Pour off excess oil.
Add onions, bell pepper, celery and water to skillet.
Cover in cooking dish.
Bake for 1 hour (depending on the size of the roast) or until tender.

seafOOD

SEAFOOD GUMBO

4 Tbls. shortening
2 Tbls. flour
1/4 cup chopped onions
1/4 cup chopped green onions
1/4 cup chopped celery
3 12 oz. cans stewed tomatoes
2 bay leaves
3 quarts of water
1/2 Tbls. salt
1/2 Tbls. crab boil
1 tsp. black pepper
1 lb. okra, cut-up
4 lbs. cleaned and deveined medium sized shrimp
1/2 dozen cleaned and shelled blue crabs (removed outer shell and guts)
    and break in half
2 lbs. real white lump crab meat

Fry okra in skillet and set aside and let cool.
Make roux (1/4 cup shortening and ¼ Cup flour) in saucepan until lightly
    brown and set aside.
Add 1lb of link sausage of choice (cut into ½ in pieces)
Pour water, stewed tomatoes, onions, pepper, celery, bay leaves and okra
    in a large pot.
Bring to a boil.
Reduce to simmer for 1 hour.
Add roux, crab boil, salt and pepper (to taste).
Add all seafood ingredients.
Simmer for 30 minutes.
Serve over rice.

FRIED CATFISH

2 lbs. catfish (fillets)
2 cups seafood fry mix
1 cup cooking oil
1/2 tsp. salt and pepper to taste

Batter fish with fry mix.
Place in cooking oil.
Fry until golden brown.
Serve.

CRAB CAKES

2 lbs. lump crab meat
1/2 cup onions
1/2 cup celery
1/2 cup bell pepper
1 cup seasoned bread crumbs
2 eggs
1/3 cup cooking oil

Mix all ingredients (except oil) together.
Make palm-sized patties and flatten.
Heat oil in cooking pan.
Fry on medium heat until golden brown.
Serve.

DeSSeRTS

TEA CAKES

1 cup of butter
2 cups of sugar
4 eggs
1 Tbl. whole milk
1 tsp. nutmeg
1 tsp. vanilla flavor
4 cups of self-rising flour (sifted 3 times)
3 Tbls. baking powder

Preheat oven at 350 degrees.
Cream butter and sugar together in mixer.
Add eggs (one at a time).
Add milk, nutmeg and flour.
Sift flour and baking powder.
Combine all ingredients.
Make dough.
Coat rolling pin with flour.
Sprinkle cooking sheet or aluminum foil with flour to prevent sticking.
Spread and roll dough out on cooking sheet (thickness to suit).
Cut with cookie cutter (sizes to suit) and place in baking dish.
Place in oven at 350 degrees.
Bake for 15 minutes.

Pies

SWEET POTATO PIE

6 regular sized sweet potatoes
3 cups sugar
1 Tbl. self-rising flour
1- 1/2 stick of Land o' Lakes Butter
6 eggs
1 tsp. nutmeg
1 tsp. butter nut flavor
1 tsp. lemon flavor
1/2 cup whipping cream
3 pie crust

Preheat oven at 300 degrees.
Boil sweet potatoes until tender, peel and then mash together.
Pour mashed potatoes into mixing bowl.
Cream butter and sugar along with mashed potatoes in mixer (low speed)
Add eggs (6) one at a time until well creamed.
Add flour and whipping cream (in alternating fashion) and continue
    to mix.
Add 1 tsp. vanilla flavor.
Add 1 tsp. lemon flavor.
Mix thoroughly.
Pour into pie crust.
Bake at 300 degrees for 1 hour.
(Recipe makes three 3 pies).

BREAD PUDDING

3 eggs beaten
1- 1/2 cup sugar
2 Tbls. light brown sugar
1/2 tsp. nutmeg
1/4 cup melted butter
2 and 3/4 cup whipping cream
4 cups bread crumbs
3/4 cup raisins

Mix all ingredients and bake at 350 degrees for 50 minutes.

BREAD PUDDING VANILLA SAUCE

1/2 cup sugar

3 Tbls. light brown sugar

1/4 tsp. of nutmeg (less nutmeg to taste)

1 tsp. flour

1 egg

2 Tbls. butter

1 1/4 cup whipping cream

1 Tbl. vanilla flavor

Mix all ingredients and cook over low heat 10-15 minutes.
Drizzle over bread pudding.

cakes

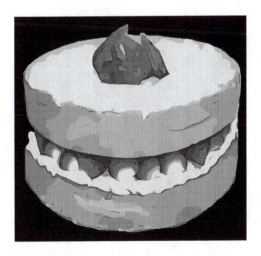

STRAWBERRY CAKE

1 box white cake mix
3 Tbls. all-purpose flour
1 package strawberry gelatin
1 cup Crisco oil
4 eggs
1/2 cup water
1/2 small bag frozen strawberries

Drain and reserve syrup from bag of strawberries.
Pour strawberries into separate bowl and set aside.
Combine cake mix, flour and gelatin and pour into mixing bowl.
Add 1 cup of cooking oil.
Begin mixing in mixer on low speed.
Add eggs (one at a time).
Add water and strawberries.
Mix well.
Bake in greased bunt pan at 350 degrees for 35-40 minutes.
Turn out onto cake plate.
Top with strawberries.

STRAWBERRY FROSTING

1/2 can frozen strawberries
1/2 stick butter (softened)
2 cups powdered sugar

Pour strawberry syrup off strawberries and set aside.
Mix all ingredients together.
Pour reserved strawberry juice (preferred consistency) over cake and spread.

RED VELVET CAKE

2 oz. red food coloring
2 tsp. cocoa (melt and make paste)
1/2 cup butter
1 1/2 cup sugar
2 eggs
2 1/2 cup cake flour
1 cup buttermilk
1 tsp. baking powder
1 tsp. vanilla flavor
1 tsp. baking soda
1 tsp. vinegar
1 tsp. salt

Preheat oven at 350 degrees.
Cream butter and sugar in mixing bowl.
Add eggs, one at a time.
Add cocoa paste; (butter, sugar, eggs and cocoa paste will make cream mixture).
Sift flour, salt and baking powder into mixing bowl (alternate with
    cream mixture).
Add flavor.
Mix baking soda and vinegar in standard sized cup (mix well).
Add baking soda and vinegar to cake batter (cream mixture).
Pour into three-layer cake pans.
Bake at 350 degrees for 30 minutes.

RED VELVET CAKE FROSTING

2 cups powdered sugar
8 oz. cream cheese
1 tsp. butter (at room temperature)
1/2 cup milk
1 cup finely chopped pecans

Mix all ingredients.
Spread over cake and serve.

CREAM CHEESE POUND CAKE

---

3 sticks butter

8 oz. cream cheese

3 cups sugar

6 eggs

3 cups cake flour

1 tsp. vanilla flavor

1 tsp. almond flavor

Preheat oven at 300 degrees.

Cream butter and cream cheese together in mixing bowl.

Add sugar.

Cream until light and fluffy.

Add eggs (one at a time).

Gradually add flour.

Add vanilla and almond flavors.

Spray cake pan with non-stick cooking spray.

Pour cake batter into cake pan.

Bake at 300 degrees for 1 and 1/2 hours.

WHIPPING CREAM POUND CAKE

1 cup butter
3 cups sugar
6 eggs
3 cups Swan's Down cake flour
1 cup whipping cream
2 tsp. pure orange extract (flavor)

Preheat oven at 300 degrees.
Set eggs and butter aside until room temperature.
Cream butter and sugar in mixer at medium speed.
Add eggs (one at a time).
Add flour and whipping cream (starting with flour alternating).
Add pure orange extract flavor.
Mix all ingredients in mixer at medium speed until batter is well creamed.
Pour into bunt cake pan.
Bake at 300 degrees for 1 and 1/2 hours in bunt pound cake pan.

CHOCOLATE CAKE

2 sticks butter
1/2 cup Crisco shortening
2 1/2 cups sugar
3 cups Swan's Down white cake flour
2 tsp. baking powder
1/3 tsp. salt
4 Tbls. cocoa powder
1 cup whole milk
1 tsp. vanilla flavor

Preheat oven at 300 degrees.
Cream butter and Crisco shortening in mixer at medium speed.
Add sugar.
Add eggs (one at a time).
Sift flour, baking powder, salt and cocoa powder (3 times).
Add flour, baking powder and cocoa powder to the above ingredients
    (alternate with milk) and mix in mixer at medium speed.
Pour into 3, layer cake pans.
Bake at 300 degrees for 30 minutes or until brown.

CHOCOLATE CAKE FROSTING

2 cups powdered sugar
3 tsp. cocoa powder
1/4 stick margarine
1 egg yolk
3/4 cup milk

Mix until creamy.
Spread over each layer.

THREE-LAYER CAKE

4 eggs
2 cups sugar
3 sticks of butter
1 cup of whole milk
Pinch of salt
3 tsp. baking powder
1 tsp. coconut flavor
1 tsp vanilla flavor
3 cups of Swan's Down All-purpose cake flower
Red food coloring
Cream cheese icing

Preheat oven at 350 degrees.
Mix coconut flavor, vanilla flavor and milk in standard sized cup and set aside.
Cream butter and sugar in mixer at medium speed.
Add eggs one at a time (mix well after each addition).
Sift flour, baking powder and salt together.
Add flour mixture, alternating with milk and flavors until creamy.
Pour 1/3 cake batter into separate bowl and set aside.
Add 3 drops of red food coloring to the separated cake batter and mix
    separately until well blended.
Grease 3 separate cooking pans with Baker's Joy.
Pour regular cake batter into two separate cake pans.
Pour red cake batter into separate cake pan.
Bake each layer in separate cake pans for 25-30 minutes.
Stack each cake layer on cake plate with red layer in the center (add cream
    cheese icing between layers).

HOMEMADE SUGAR SYRUP

2 cups sugar
2 cups of water
3 quart boiler

Put sugar into boiler.
Bring sugar to a light brown bubble (brown around the edges of the sugar).
Pour in water; cook until lightly thick.
Remove from heat.

PReSeRVeS

FIG-PEAR-PEACH PRESERVES

1 gallon rinsed, peeled and sliced fruit (figs should remain whole)
5 lbs. sugar
1 box Sure Gel
2 lemons, sliced (remove seeds from lemons, pears and peaches)
One large pot
Standard mason jars with lids and seals (enough to contain cooked preserves)

Pour fruit into large bowl.
Cover with sugar.
Let stand overnight or for 6-7 hours. (Sugar will melt and make syrup).
Put on high heat and add lemons and Sure Gel.
Cook on high for 10 minutes.
Turn heat to lowest and stir occasionally.
Cook until syrup thickens.
Heat jars and lids in large pot of boiling water before filling with preserves.
Pour hot preserves into hot mason jars and seal. (This will help preserves seal).

Printed in the United States
by Baker & Taylor Publisher Services